God Call / God Order

by Valorie Tatum

www.WeAreAPS.com

"The Bible is the story of two gardens: Eden and Gethsemane.

In the first, Adam took a fall.
In the second, Jesus took a stand.
In the first, God sought Adam.
In the second, Jesus sought God.
In Eden, Adam hid from God.
In Gethsemane, Jesus emerged from the tomb.
In Eden, the serpent lured Adam to a tree that led to his death.
From Gethsemane, Jesus went to a tree that led to our life".

Max Lucado

Author's Note

One day I sat in church looking and listening to the sermon. The pastor happened to mention some key words (Laity Role in the church) that sent me on a new prayer journey for my life. We all in some form or another have served on a committee or two in our home churches, but do we clearly understand why we serve and what the steps tare o being a good servant to others? Is it my calling, my duty, my responsibility or my brother and sister's keeper?

I have been reading and taking a confirmation class under the leadership of my pastor to determine my calling. The reading of The Christian as Minister: An Exploration into the Meaning of God's Call will be the guide of writing and reflection in which my own book is based on along with other spiritual resources.

Table of Contents

Chapter 1 – The Call

When did it happen? Who have you told? How do you know it is truly meant for you? We have and are now living in a century that exhibits a compelling quality that evokes reflection more than ever into self.

What has been and from where we have come in more than 2000 years of our God's history. This has placed us and propelled us between backward and forward of a long list of possibilities for the future - not only of self in the ministry, but the church as well.

The church has always been in the mainstream of our society's priorities. It is also the economic, social and political forces which contribute to the have and have-nots, the handling of diversity in the realm of people and money. This challenges us to examine our relationship with God, the call/the order in new ways. The church is supposed to be building and equipping Christians to go out into the world to pray; to be resourceful and help those in need utilizing the Bible as our means of responding to the masses.

Rationale for My Mission

My rationale or my mission is in conjunction with the Methodist Church Mission. The mission is to make disciples of Jesus Christ by proclaiming the good news of God's grace... thus seeking the fulfillment of God's reign and realm in the world. The fulfillment of God's reign and realm in the world is the vision scripture holds before us. The United Methodist Church affirms that Jesus Christ is the Son of God, the Savior of the world and the Lord of all. We respect persons of all religious faiths and we defend religious freedom for all persons. Jesus' words in Matthew provide the church with our mission: "Therefore go and make disciples of all notions, baptizing them in the name of the Father and the Son and the Holy Spirit, teaching them to obey everything that I've commanded you.." (28:19-20)

The textual evidence is seen throughout the Bible that the Reign of God in the world as announced by Jesus. God's grace is active everywhere at all times. God made a covenant with Abraham and Sarah. In Exodus, he made one with the children of Israel in delivering them from Egypt.

And yet another in the ministry of the prophets. John Wesley, Phllip Otterbeing, Jacob Albright and our other spiritual fore-bearers understood this mission in this way.

The key is for the church to do the following: save persons; heal relationships (with God's words and not our own God complex); transform social structures (capacity building, restorative building); and spread spiritual holiness (not the Iyanla Vanzant complex).

Chapter 2 – Reflections with Jesus

In what ways have I experienced the church as a faith community in my life? The church has always been the key to my life as far back as my birth. When I awake on Sunday mornings, I am confronted with mortality. I sleep, but we never know when we will ever wake up again or if we are guaranteed to live another day.

The church (not the temple, but the people) has always been part of my life because of the uniqueness of the church - it is comprised of my biological family. They are a mixture of what I will be and what I have encountered in the world. They are part of what I am and what I hope not to be all the time.

The faith community I live in knows how to surrender our selfish desires and we watch the embers of that old life crumble into ash. We have supported through prayers, conversations, challenges and changes to still strive in a time of brokenness. The faith community offers a vision of peace, strength, order, wholeness and unity, which is in conjunction with what God wills for all creation.

What are the ways I have experienced the church as a response to the societal and political forces which exclude, alienate and marginalize others? My mission, along with that of the United Methodist mission, is to make sure the church adheres to the needs of those in our community. We accomplish this through serving meals to the poor; providing clothing pantries; teaching the word; and networking with sources to provide safe, responsible and respectable health services.

The United Methodist is governed by the book of discipline that sets the guidelines for running our ministries and organizations to work effectively for the love and safety of all persons that enter our doors. We meet to discuss topics, and resolve conflicts of spiritual interest world wide not just locally.

My understanding agrees with the church's mission. I believe that once God sees his people working to carry out his mission to save persons, heal relationships, transform social structures and spread spiritual holiness, it will thereby change the world. We have met and exceeded the tolerance of each other and demonstrated that love for each other. When the have and have-nots are replaced to not only balance, but become equal, we will have embraced Jesus' mandate because we are the church through Him.

Chapter 3 – The Call

Water, a precious commodity. Wading, splashing, drinking and healing with it. So, why baptism? Baptism is a gift from God; it is unmerited grace in conjunction with the holy spirit, the mark that draws and brings us into the church. Understand that once you clarify your calling it will not always be affirmed by the people on the street or the people of God.

Jesus knew this all too well as shown in the text when Jesus went to Nazareth. Jesus went to Nazareth, where He had been raised. On the Sabbath, He went to the synagogue as He normally did and stood up to read. The synagogue assistant gave him the scroll from the prophet Isaiah. He unrolled the scroll and found the place where it was written: "The Spirit of the Lord is upon me, because the Lord has anointed me. He has sent me to preach good news to the poor, to proclaim release to the prisoners and recovery of sight to the blind, to liberate the oppressed and to proclaim the year of the Lord's favor." He rolled up the scroll, gave it back to the synagogue assistant, and sat down. Every eye in the synagogue was fixed on him.

He began to explain to them: "Today this scripture has been fulfilled just as you heard it." Everyone was raving about Jesus, so impressed were they by the gracious words flowing from his lips. They said, "This is Joseph's son, isn't it?" Then Jesus said to them, "Undoubtedly, you will quote this saying to me: Doctor, heal yourself. Do here in your hometown what we've heard you did in Capernaum."

He said, "I assure you that no prophet is welcome in the prophet's hometown." When they heard this, everyone in the synagogue was filled with anger. They rose up and ran him out of town. They led him to the crest of the hill on which their town had been built so that they could throw him off the cliff. But he passed through the crowd and went on his way. (Luke 4:16-24: 28-30)

Chapter 4 – Reflections with Jesus

As part of Christ's family, signified by my baptism, what does being a lay/minister of the world in Christ's name mean to me? I have found that my calling and Jesus' calling have a lot in common. He struggled with vocational choices as do I. I know the spirit of the Lord is upon me, my life to this point has been guided and protected by God's will for me. I have tried to deny it but every way, every day and every destination has been guided and referenced to God. It is truly not a set time, situation, or highlighted detail that determine when it will happen, it just does.

God is a precise God, a capacity building, a robust strategist that leaves nothing to chance. And when you are called, it is not just by chance, but by His will for you. We have had trials and tribulations that try to trick us away but the calling is so deep in the spirit that no matter what, you will come to it by choice with a powerful force.

What work will God have me do in the name of Christ, for the sake of the world? A statement that caught my eye as I studied during my confirmation class was the following: In a way, your vocation in life grows out of His because Christ invites you.

I went to college to major in Business Law and Psychology. I never thought I would be a teacher like Jesus. I have now been a teacher for twenty years at the time I started writing this book. I still to this day think back and say, "This was a God move and not a Valorie move". I never thought that I would work with children – especially those with disabilities. Like Jesus' experience, it has had its struggles and rewards.

Today, the scripture and ministry God has for me is moving in the path He desires and not just what I desire. I am not insinuating that I am holier than thou, but there is an order I follow along with some strong prayer that helps me move into what both God and I have come to desire for the outcome of my life.

What kind of ministry might God call me to that would require my total obedience? My mother was an electrician and my father was a construction worker. Choosing a ministry or leadership position required some self-reflection and self-surveying to find my gifts especially because I was not sure what they were. We often choose things where we excel and move away from or step outside of the box for challenging positions.

Gifts in ministry often reflect the systematic way of the pro and con elevating process. Church folk will often put ourselves in positions that don't appear to require much work. They hold a position without fully understanding the responsibilities that accompany taking it. I stay in prayer, as I believe that I have been serving as a lay servant with outreach responsibilities in and outside the church/community. I have encountered a lot of work with physical, and behavioral health.

Does this mean I'm able to discover the lifework or vocation that I believe God intends for me? I am working in the church and providing financial support to meet the needs of hunger adherence, HIV/AIDS educational support, pastoral lay servant duties, writing about my journey, and being an eyewitness to the community. I have also served as youth

director for a nonprofit, youth program.
So, what are my next steps?

Chapter 5 - The Call

Clearly and simply put, my next steps are to understand the heart of Christian ministry and share Christ's love in the world. The ministry of any laity should be the front and most important reflection of that love. It is not by mere super hero powers that we come into our gifts and talents, but by God knowing us first.

The responsibilities cannot and should not be delegated and/or given if Christians are not committed to working in love and faith when engaging and developing new ministries for the church and/or community. It is a challenge to negotiate relationships, and understanding your spiritual gifts is no cake walk. There are different spiritual gifts, but the same spirit. We are all on the same journey. Even if our gifts are different, the same spirit should be evident both in the physical and spirit of the work.

It has been also identified as a privilege and a responsibility. God is the great I Am and we as humans with all our fallacies are God's own possession and after His heart. It is no joke when we are called to respond to God's calling; it is a great responsibility and obedience to Christ. It provides us total growth and nurturing in order to grow spiritually to mature in our Christian life.

It has been also identified as a privilege and a responsibility. God is the great I Am and we as humans with all our fallacies are God's own possession and after His heart. It is no joke when we are called to respond to God's calling; it is a great responsibility and obedience to Christ. It provides us total growth and nurturing in order to grow spiritually to mature in our Christian life.

It is through our congregational understanding of John Wesley's General Rules for the Societies that help us as Methodist to pray, worship, and watch over one another in love and serving God's children. We can do this by first understanding and doing no harm and avoiding evil of every kind.

My own community of Englewood has suffered greatly because of the lack of understanding this process and establishing clear boundaries of how to effectively execute as the community transitions through generational disparities. Second, doing good on every level and to every person, this requires others to understand and move beyond self. It is very difficult to this when self has not met its own needs or treated itself with good.

Our lives have become "get more, need more, and I think I'm entitled to more" living. The third issue that highlights what it takes to do ministry in God's way and not ours is how we stay connected to Him. We run from God because we do not want to take responsibility for our own mistakes. It is easier to say God did it instead of confronting the man in the mirror. What did I do? How can I change that? Who can help me? Did I seek God in all aspects of my situation?

Chapter 6 - Reflections with Jesus

Think about unique gifts you may have to relate to young people who are making vocational decisions about their future. Are you uniquely suited to work with college students, faculty and staff of all ages to help them grow in their faith development? Are you comfortable relating to people of all faiths, or those who profess no faith, in an academic environment?

I have been teaching in Chicago Public Schools for 22 years in the area of Special Education and it has turned out to be a valid and valued calling. It is and has continued to be a ministry of importance, although it is extremely challenging and unpredictable on all levels of social, economic and religious concerns.

This vocational decision has always been a God call and not a Valorie choice of profession or ministry. The goals are to make disciples of Jesus Christ; to grow and strengthen congregations and their communities; to alleviate human suffering; and to promote justice, peace, and freedom to the masses of the world. What better place to start than in an elementary school with our children - God's children?

It is no secret that the Chicago Public Schools has become a pool of severely emotional, and economic games of injustice for the rich politicians. It is clear at an alarming rate that our children are falling through the cracks of hopelessness of becoming and being the productive citizens this country has built its foundational constitutional laws upon.

It is no secret that the church and state have been disconnected for many decades, with everyone in its place and no place for children to balance themselves. It has been publicized how the basis of nonprofit organizations are now being housed in many of the churches in many communities across the city. The church has found its niche in a place that has disconnected itself from church being in the place of academic.

The nonprofits have made ministries for church laity to begin responding to the call to mission service in many ways. Pastors are talking with principals, parents, unions and school leadership to open their doors to support children and their home environments through various outreach programs. This can be done to address the family spiritual needs, ongoing behavioral needs, economic needs and parental training needs.

Chapter 7 - The Call

Do you really feel called or are you going through a phase of changes? If you feel called talk with your pastor or clergy person. Think clearly and research the call, through observations, volunteer work, shadow programs, and/or available internships before making the commitment. So, consider the following when you make that spiritual vocational choice. Refer back to your gifts, your passion, your daily living, your career path, your devotional life and your prayers. Most importantly, listen for God's voice and guidance as He will reveal things when you are being still and listening to him.

Consider the things in your life you want most but are afraid you will not get. What if it *does* work out? What will that look like? What actions can you take that will demonstrate you arc operating in faith rather than fear? We often say that fear is part of us because we are human, however, this is contradictory to when God says, "I have not given a spirit of fear". So we should not be operating our lives in fear.

In reading our Devotional Life, I have noted some key aspects. It is clearly defined that whatever ministry role we take, we must be prepared and fit for leadership. This includes learning the Bible, taking Bible study courses, carving daily time for reading and reflecting scripture, and seeking support to interpret scripture.

I also have found the role of studying theology and its role with the Bible and implementation effective for understanding the Bible. Being steadfast in prayer is an area that demands great commitment and the reverence of being still to listen to God directions and directives for your life. Discerning in prayer requires your time, energy and commitment and the support of others to help discern what leadership you will take and how effective you will be in its role.

Chapter 8 - Reflections with Jesus

The leadership of the laity has a long history in the United Methodist Denomination. The Pastors and Lay Members have had joint roles in keeping the congregational ministry going. My role in the Lay Leadership began in my family church, also with United Methodist; I possessed an overwhelming feeling to serve.

It began as early as my teenage years being an Usher, later Sunday School Teacher and Superintendent of Sunday School, Choir member, Women's Board member, and the last 8 years as the Chairperson of Pastor Parish Board, and Church Council Secretary. My current position is Lay Leader/Servant at the local level.

Some resources I've found interesting to support my journey for ministry are the following: Accountable Discipleship Living in God's Household, Steven W. Manskar, Discipleship Resources (www.gbod.org/covenantdiscipleship), that support covenant discipleship group work.

It is no easy task for Lay Leaders/Lay Servants and Lay Speakers to be prepared for church life and the responsibilities as they mimic the role of the pastor.

We must assess our spiritual gifts; profess members; read the guidelines for effective leadership in our roles; and know what the book of discipline says concerning our roles in the church. We must also become certified in the highest levels of this role so that we are implementers of our roles with the word of God and rules/policies governing the doctrine of the United Methodist Boundaries.

Chapter 9 - The Order

I am currently taking a Confirmation Class to better evaluate my call, but understanding the order of that call. The study and the research will enable me to better think of where I am and if I really need to move further in the role and what the role will continue to require of me as I grow each year. I will be utilizing excerpts and descriptions from the book, The Christian as Minister: An Exploration into the Meaning of God's Call, a book being used in my class at this time.

Lay Member to Annual Conference have the responsibility to represent their congregation at an annual conference and help interpret the actions and activities of the annual conference to their congregations. Now for me to consider moving into this position from where I am, I have things to consider. I am currently a professing member of the United Methodist Church and have been for more than two years, and I've been active in the United Methodist for more than four years. If I apply, I do have a great chance of being elected by the charge conference to annual conference for the year of 2018.

The Lay Leader, The Lay Servant, and Lay Speaker functions range as representatives to the local church, district or annual conference in which through their charge conferences are elected. They are given gifts to work very closely with the pastor in their needs, the church needs and supporting sermons, worship and church meeting with various committees.

Currently, I am appointed to my church's nomination team, which is how I provide servant leadership. I work in worship service, providing scripture reading, worship order, and sermon topics. I'm researching ways to improve my role. One way is to complete confirmation classes to advance my duties to the annual conference level.

Additionally, I can advance structure of how we do charity and outreach in our churches and community. I have two years to decide whether to become a deacon in the United Methodist Church. Meeting the qualifications for the office of Deaconess is not easy as this will be a lifetime call and mission that must be built upon yearly.

The call will definitely require the person to be called from God and will require prayer and listening to God before starting the process. Membership in the United Methodist Church must be evident. The professional training education and commissioning must be approved at the church level in vocational and/or helping service.

The individual must be able to actively practice the ability of discernment. The person must work in studies of biblical practice interpretations; theological core studies; sociological core studies that are reflective and balanced with the Old Testament; New Testament; Theology Mission; History of the United Methodist, Polity and Doctrine of the United Methodist Church.

Reflecting on The God Call/ God Order element of becoming the servant God wants and working effectively in the ministry and mission for my life surrounds a great deal of love. My Sunday School teachings for example, challenge me in the area of loving self, loving others and loving God. My ministry and mission will not be complete unless these areas are well-balanced for the call.

The source of all love is to know that God is love and that His love is not restrained, restricted, or false. It is constant, consistent, challenging, and eternal without boundaries. It is revealed in us, his son, Jesus, those in the past, and future followers.

The beginning of these lessons are in the root of 1 John 4:7-19, "Dear friends, let's love each other, because love is from God and everyone who loves is born from God and knows God. The person who doesn't love does not know God, because God is love. This is how the love of God is revealed to us; God has sent his only Son into the world so that we can live through him. This is love; it is not that we loved God but that he loved us and sent his Son as the sacrifice that deals with our sins".

Dear friends, if God loved us this way, we also ought to love each other. No one has ever seen God. If we love each other, God remains in us and his love is made perfect in us. This is how we know we remain in him and he remains in us, because he has given us a measure of his Spirit. We have seen and testify that the Father has sent the Son to be the savior of the world.

If any of us confess that Jesus is God's Son, God remains in us and we remain in God.

We have known and have believed the love that God has for us. God is love, and those who remain in love remain in God and He remains in them. This is how love has been perfected in us, so that we can have confidence on the Judgment Day, because we are exactly the same as God is in this world. There is no fear in love, but perfect love drives out fear, because fear expects punishment. The person who is afraid has not been made perfect in love. We love because God first loved us.

So, if God loves and loved us this way, we ought to move into our ministry and mission with love for self and others. This is the key to moving into your future with God with little or no reservations, no fears, no concerns, trusting to be led by Him and the Holy Spirit. Throughout my time in the church, what have I learned from Jesus about his ministry and mission, about his relationship with God and his life here on earth that will give me what I want and need to do his work?

Do some people need God's love more than others? Before answering, we must first clearly understand that grace is God's free gift of saving love. With that said, would you agree or disagree that some need more love? Do you think that God's love should be accepted without putting a stipulation of how much is needed?

This is my belief, as God's love is freely given. It is immeasurable, yet is capable of handling exactly what is needed in all our situations, trials and tribulations. No tricks are needed, no added obligations, no additional actions necessary to call on God's love. It is sufficient to do what it is given for through your faith. He doesn't love any one of his children less than the other; therefore, his love is balanced to meet the need of each of us according to our needs not less nor more. His love is balanced, and perfectly equipped to meet our need.

Is faith something that we do, something that God does, or something we do together with God? I believe that faith is something we do together with God; it is action, can be implemented and has results. It is prevenient grace, already placed with you for God to work through you in the necessary condition. It is revealed to be activated for the serving of the kingdom.

What am I doing for God now that will lift up the kingdom? My writing has moved more to spiritual writing and critiquing. I first starting writing children books, but have found that I'm on my third spiritual journey book.

In what ways do I stay connected with Jesus? It is important to identify the qualities that define your relationship with God and His love. John 15:1-8,
"I am the true vine, and my father is the vineyard keeper. He removes any of my branches that don't produce fruit, and he trims any branch that produces fruit so that it will produce even more fruit. You are ready trimmed because of the word I have spoken to you. Remain in me, and I will remain in you. A branch can't produce fruit by itself, but must remain in the vine. Like wise you can't produce fruit unless you remain in me. I am the vine; you are the branches. If you remain in me and I in you, then you will produce much fruit. Without me you can't do anything. If you don't remain in me, you will be like a branch that is thrown out and dries up. Those branches are gathered up, thrown

into a fire, and burned. If you remain in me and my words remain in you. Ask for whatever you want and it will be done for you. My Father is glorified when you produce much fruit and in this way prove that you are my disciples."

How many times have we done things in disgrace? I remember the people of Israel felt disgraced because the locust were a great sign from God that they had been disobedient. Like a child, we can have that same feeling of shame, and punishment being so overwhelming that we didn't know how to talk about or emotionally come back from it.

Is misfortune a sign that God is displeased with us? I have found that as humans, we associate everything bad with God when it's simply a unique instance of human sufferings. God made this world for us but we are not of this world, so its tragedies have to be clearly identified for what it is, why it happens and where it really comes from.

The key no matter the situation, is to understand that trial and tribulation help you grow closer to God; you should not turn away from Him in the time of crisis. Yes, you may feel unworthy, undeserving, lost, unloved and afraid, but God's love is steadfast. It brings changes; it uplifts capacity building and sustainability through any trial, tribulation or outcome.

Now, for repentance. I have learned in these 38 years of reflection, self assessment, and working through me that yes, there is a case for repentance in your life whether you want it or not. You must ask, "How has my relationship with God changed over time? Can I identify particular events in my life that provided occasions for turning points? I can begin the list at age 12: my mother sick; brother murdered; father dead; grandparents dead; favorite cousin murdered; sister on drugs (Hosanna most high - she's been drug free for close to 17 years); financial struggles; and it has been seasons of my own medical surges.

I have had those points of feeling alone but not lonely, scared but not lost, shaken but healed and recovered, hindered but continued to move forward. Relationships can not be repaired if both parties can't see the damage. God knows.

the damage is open to repairs and has the best possible solutions.

Chapter 10 - Reflections with Jesus

I want to up lift one of my favorite scriptures: It is the claim on what it means to trust God. Psalm 23, "The Lord is my shepherd, I lack nothing. He lets me rest in grassy meadows: he leads me to restful waters: he keeps me alive. He guides me in proper paths for the sake of his good name. Even when I walk through the darkest valley, I fear no evil because you are with me. Your rod and staff, they protect me. You set a table for me right in front of my enemies. You bathe my head with oil: my cup runs over! Yes, goodness and mercy shall pursue me all the days of my life and I will live in the lord's house all my days."

The Lord Is My Shepherd:
He sees me as the individual, being one with him, living, worshipping and spiritually growing. It comes a time that each of us must engage in our faith that changes often but not too quickly for God.

We as mere humans connect everything we say, do and have to our jobs, current experiences, faith and God. We must recognize our position with God not above, nor below but in connection, trusting God to do His work; our work is to pray for our fellow man.

I always let family, friends and others know my name is not Iyanla - I can't fix what it takes God to change, but I will pray and provide resources to support the journey. I must know my position that I cannot make another person trust in God. We must identify our own struggles in trusting God and seek friends, clergy and God to regain help in reclaiming that trust.

I Shall Not Want:

Everything I have is in God. Failure to trust God has become a serious reason for us replacing God with things. I found that I, as well as others, however rich or poor or in between, have all experienced nontrivial lack and nontrivial awareness of lack in our lives. It is seen in how we feel about our bodies, homes, jobs, children and spiritual life.

The best way to deal with this is to inventory what you have, what you think you need and then spring clean both of the concepts. When you feel lack, confess to God your concerns and troubles believing that you have everything you need and want. God is the one you trust, to be trustworthy with you and to provide what is the deficit.

In Green Pastures:
I believe this is a time of not walking through the garden of human touch, but of God's love. God's presence is so powerful during our trials and tribulation that we think we are carrying it ourselves because of such strong strength.

The truth is that He is near us, loving us, collaborating and communing with us on all scales of trauma letting us know that we are not alone. The moments are for his hearing, for opening up to feel his breath, his thoughts, his touch, and his feelings of embracing the situation. We become his babies that he holds and attend too in every possible way we can relate, meeting us at our needs.

The Valley of the Shadow of Death:
It is no cake walk for any man, woman, or child. It has its impacts on low and high marginal scales and sometimes recovery is not often evident. We see this at funerals, shocking death experiences and

the media. The truth is that most of us are looking at death through different lenses for various reasons. We may not have had a relationship with the dead for a long time. The times we feel bad because we may perceive ones death as a blessing more than a loss. This doesn't mean that we are not suffering the loss, rather the phase of grieving simply may not be acceptable to others.

Chapter 11 - The Order

The following chapters will discuss the process of self analysis - who we are; what we want; and how to use simple tools of honesty, and synthesizing to become the desired outcome of the person we want to be.

It is clear that the questioning and answering must clearly support gifts, capacity of rate building and sustainability that can be measured by academic self and social self. In our lifetime we have read many self-reflection and self-help books to become a better person. I think it is important to include the questions that help put our goal(s) in reasonable, and workable achievement in order to become the better you and make life growth to become what we want to do in living according to God's outcomes for us.

I have some vital thoughts on measuring progress in whatever goal(s) you are working on in a year and or years to become who and what you want to be and do. I have utilized these four questions throughout my life and when I am writing books: *What goal(s) are most successful this year or within the last six months?* I have found finishing my books to be the key to answering this question.

What is the success of the goal(s) this year or the last six months? I have been able to utilize the book success to support much needed community resources.

What about the success of this goal(s) are most important to building on to your future goal(s)? I have thought about moving more into Christian outreach and or becoming a deacon in the church and this is a vital success because it places me in a position to view the needs of the community and much needed resources.

What tools will help you reach the new goal(s) and be easier to work on in a less stressful manner? This will require research for volunteer, financial and networking to ensure the process is utilized by capacity building of support systems that can run the goal with and without your being there all the time.

Chapter 12 - Reflections with Jesus

I want to reflect back on the importance of time with God. I can only say how important and necessary it is to implement these reflections. The success of all we are, all we do, and who we are doing it for depends on God.

Key things to remember and to take measuring progress on are the following. How can I make sure the scheduling conflicts are adequately and supportively going to be worked out? Do my life and goals build consistency, sustainability, and capacity or are they short lived with no room for growth? Have I removed the emotional and financial obstacles that can hurt me?

We must also take a look at the connections we are making to those that will be part of the process. This is not an easy step because everyone can not accompany you on your journey. When talking to God, discuss how to incorporate space, energy and time so as not to grow weary. Christians often discuss how tired we are and we don't know when to stop and when to begin and the process can quickly become overwhelming.

Finally, when talking to God, do a quick beginning, mid year and projected ending year review of positive and negative emotions, finances and goal progress, then establish your focus for the remaining year.

Chapter 13 - The Call/The Order

      In this chapter, I want to discuss strength. I would like to focus on how God can call us to do something way before our time. It can happen even in the womb. Let's take a look at Samson, yes called in the womb, even though he struggled with his goal to be what God needed him to be. Samson's call is used to demonstrate and remember that God created each person for a purpose that may not go together with our own choosing.

      Judges 13:1-7, 24-25

      "The Israelites again did things that the Lord saw as evil, and he handed them over to the Philistines for forty years. Now there was a certain man from Zorah, from the Danite clan, whose name was Manoah. His wife was unable to become pregnant and had not given birth to any children. The Lord's messenger appeared to the woman and said to her, "Even though you've been unable to become pregnant and haven't given birth, you are now pregnant and will give birth to a son! Now be careful not to drink wine or brandy or to eat anything that is ritually unclean, because you are pregnant and will give birth to a son. Don't allow a razor to shave his head, because the boy is going to be a Nazarite for God from birth. He'll be the one who begins Israel's rescue from the power of the Philistines." Then the woman went and told her husband, "A man of God came to me, and he looked liked God's messenger-very scary! I didn't ask him where he was from, and he didn't tell me his name. He said to me, 'You are pregnant and will give birth to a son, so don't drink wine or brandy or eat anything that is ritually unclean, because the boy is going to be a Nazarite for God from birth until the day he dies.' ... The woman gave birth to a son and named him Samson. The boy grew up, and the Lord Blessed him. The Lord's spirit began to move him whe he was in Mahaneh-dan, between Zorah and Eshtaol."

The word "begins" is important to remember in this scripture when reading further into Judges and the goals and life of Samson. He was a great warrior when completing his task for God and was able to bring many years of rest for his people from under the Philistine rule. Looking at Samson helps determine the kind of strength needed to be not weary in well doing for God and his outcomes for me.

Understand that Samson's character is totally different from what we would expect from someone God would use as a deliverer. Judges reveals Samson as a man who was impulsive, violent, prone to rage, arrogant, and reluctant to lead. This is any child of God on any given day - including me. These are reflections of our behaviors when we are called to the call and to the order of God. Yet Samson was the one God chose, and as for us, we are made in his image, given his breath and his inheritance.

Chapter 14 - The Response

I believe God chose me for a specific purpose. I believe things in my life I did not choose for myself. I believe I have received above adequate preparation for the tasks and special gifts to meet the call/order and the challenge to face what He has for me. I believe God always keeps His presence with me even when I'm in struggle and acceptance roles. I know that I can trust him. I know that my uniqueness will be unfolded for the right time and place to be of service.

What questions must be answered as I believe and know that there is a calling on my life. How will I respond to the calling? Am I willing to follow, and trust God's wisdom and follow his divine instructions? Do you have the strength to believe that God will stand with you as he did with Samson even when you rebel? Can you forgive and move on and turn to God for repentance?

This prayer is very connective for me, it is one we studied in our Sunday School class. "God, the source of all wisdom, give us the courage to accept the calls you have placed on our lives and the circumstances in which you have placed us to live out those calls. Keep us faithful, and grant us forgiveness when we are not. When we doubt our purpose or lose our way, hold us close, and set us on the right path. Use us in your service: in Jesus name I/we pray. Amen."

Chapter 15 – Final Call/Final Order

Calling all God's saints and servants meeting with the Burning Bush, the almighty God. It is now time to recognize God's presence as we partner to correct the injustices that plague our communities, cities, country and world. This is a time when I am glad that my Sunday school lessons are shedding insight into my desire to move more into my calling.

I live in the Englewood Community in Chicago, a community heavily plagued with violence, financial struggles and loss of family connections/roots. It reminds me of the story of Moses and the Burning Bush. The struggle of the Israelites, cries of oppression and injustice by the Egyptians that had been heard by God.

Exodus 3:1-12

Moses was taking care of the flock for his father -in-law Jethro, Midian's priest. He led his flock out to the edge of the desert, and he came to God's mountain called Horeb. The Lord's messenger appeared to him in a flame of fire in the middle of a bush. Moses saw that the bush was in flames, but it didn't burn up. Then Moses said to himself, "Let me check out this amazing sight and find out why the bush isn't burning up". When the Lord saw that he was coming to look, God called to him out of the bush, "Moses, Moses!"

Moses said, "I'm here." Then the Lord said, "Don't come any closer! Take off your sandals, because you are standing on holy ground." He continued, "I am the God of your father, Abraham's God, Isaac's God, and Jacob's God." Moses hid his face because he was afraid to look at God.

Then the Lord said, "I've clearly seen my people oppressed in Egypt. I've heard their cry of injustice because of their slave masters. I know about their pain. I've come down to rescue them from the Egyptians in order to take them out of the land and bring them to a good and broad land, a land that's full of milk and honey, a place where the Canaanites, the Hittites, the Amorites, the Perizzites, the Hivites, and Jebusites all live.

Now the Israelites' cries of injustice have reached me. I've seen just how much the Egyptians have oppressed them. So get going, I'm sending you to Pharaoh to bring my people, the Israelites, out of Egypt."

But Moses said to God, "Who am I to go to Pharaoh and to bring the Israelites out of Egypt?"

God said, "I'll be with you. This will show you that I'm the one who sent you. After you bring the people out of Egypt, you will come back here and worship God on this mountain."

So when I think about this story, I find it to be a perfect analogy for my life. I live in Englewood, a community oppressed in the same manner as the Israelites. Many times I wonder, "Who am I to go and stand up for these people?" However, I realize that God has a calling on all of us to lead the oppressed, sick, and the helpless.

Find your purpose and partner with Him for your place. God said he would be with his leaders, saints and children especially to help the meek and lowly. So, when he calls will you say, "I'm here" or will you continue to rebel? I've chosen to answer the call.

Other Books by Valorie Tatum

Rita Rabbit and the Runaway Pie

Once Upon A Time I was Never Young

Who Would You Tell:
A Guide to Help Overcome Bullying

Beyond Being Valorie: A Healing Journey

Corresponding Journals are also available

39956720R00033

Made in the USA
Middletown, DE
25 March 2019